The Cat on the Track

illustrations with thanks to Canva

This book is dedicated to my Husband

Robert

There's a cat on the track
the railway track...

He's walking into town

There's a cat on the track
the railway track...

and the rain is pouring down!

There's a cat on the track
with stripes on his back

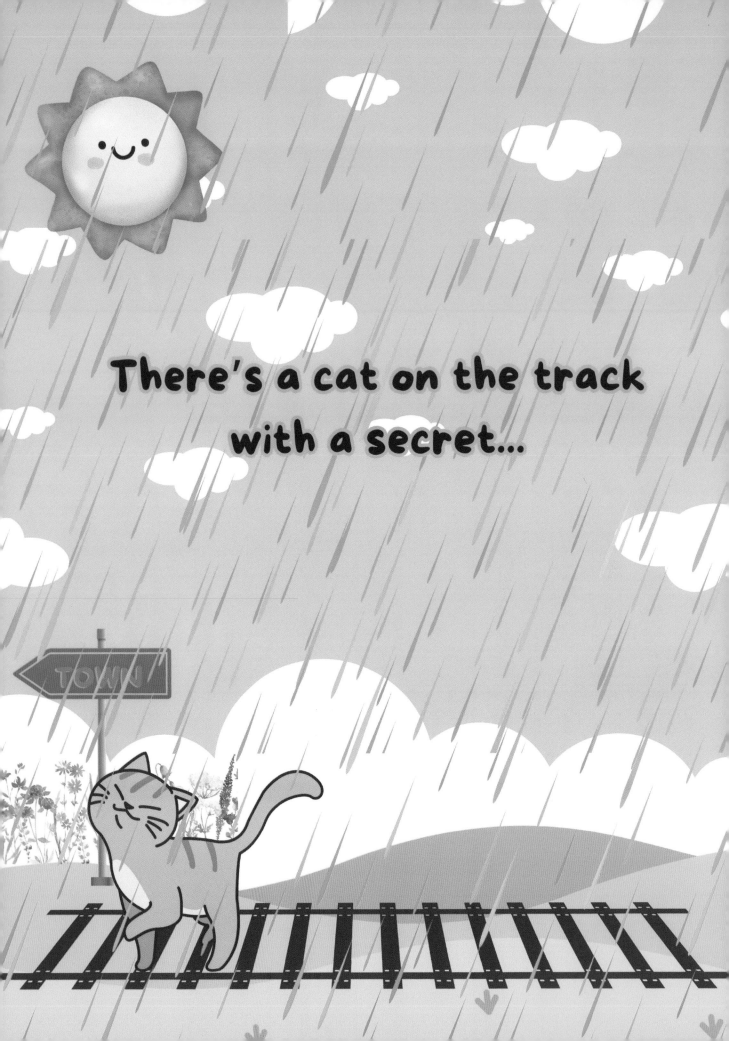

There's a cat on the track
with a secret...

and he wont tell me nor you!

There's a cat on the track
the railway track...

and a train is on its way

You can see it in the distance...

but the cat decides to stay!

There's a cat on the track
the railway track...

and he's got to get off fast!

The train is moving closer and the cat must let it pass!

There's a train on the track
the railway track...

and the cat has disappeared

He's wandered off to safety
so it's not what we have
feared!!

The railway track is quiet
and the sun's come out to play

But who's that quietly walking
now the train is far away?

There's a cat on the track
the railway track

and he's there all
safe and sound

There's a cat on the track
the railway track...

and he's walking into town!

What's this?
There's TWO on the track
the railway track...

walking back from town

There's two
by the track
the railway track
together and lying down!

Printed in Great Britain
by Amazon